PRICE OBJECTION HANDLING MADE EASY

PRICE OBJECTION HANDLING MADE EASY

118 PROVEN SALES TACTICS

that never leave you speechless in a price negotiation

ROMAN KMENTA

IMPRINT

READERS' COMMENTS

"The bad feeling when the customer questions the price and says, 'too expensive,' I know only too well. Then for the first time: speechless. It's good to have a guide to action or, even better, lots of ready-made sentences. As always with Roman Kmenta, 100% practice-relevant and immediately applicable. I tried it - it simply makes you feel good to have the answers in your head during the conversation. Speechless was yesterday!"

"Maria Husch, Die Raumexpertin
www.mariahusch.com

"Really great! - Roman Kmenta is a true expert all around the price! Anyone who is unsure about pricing and the price they are worth, his E-book will definitely help!"

René Klampfer, Geschäftsführer Skillswerk
www.skillswerk.at

"Roman Kmenta is one of the most likeable price strategists on the market! In his latest E-book, he reveals his best tips and tricks on how to enforce your price successfully and permanently. Pointedly and with many examples, he explains different methods of dealing with objections and how to turn prejudices into advantages. Small book - great value!"

Dr. Roman Szeliga, Humorexperte
www.roman-szeliga.com

TABLE OF CONTENT

Imprint 4

Readers' comments...5

Table of content...7

How you benefit from this book.....................................17

Notes on the third, expanded edition 19

Never be speechless again 20

"Too expensive" and its relatives 21

Expensive or too expensive 23

The objection-handling must fit the pricing strategy.....24

How to successfully handle objections 27

The most common mistakes when dealing with objections 27

Handling objections - how it works 29

118 variants of handling objections of "too expensive" 33

Rejection and withdrawal 33

1.   That's a pity; I thought we were going to do business......... 34

2.   We can talk about everything but the price!......................34

3.   No! You can't because ... .34

Bonus 1: I'll tell you right up front, you won't want me..................37

Evasion 38

4.   Ignore and do not react at all..38

5.   *I see, so you find the price is higher than expected. Can I ask you a question? What do you think about the build quality?* 38

Bonus 2: Oh, one more thing just came to mind. Is the tire dimension right for you? 39

Reframing or reinterpretation 40

6.   *So you think the price is still not quite what you want.* 40

7.   *Did you want something CHEAPER?* 41

8.   *The fact that you ask me for a lower price means that you want it. Do I see that right?* 41

9.   *Right! It is a valuable product!* 41

10.   *Thank you for your feedback. So that means you still need more information to properly assess the value for you?* 43

11.   *That means it is only about 100 € more than you originally wanted to spend.* 43

Bonus 3: It all depends on what is important to you and what you are trying to achieve. Many of my clients choose it BECAUSE it looks and is expensive, and that's a deciding factor in how it looks to the outside world. 43

Agree 44

12.   *True. As is so often the case, quality has its price.* 44

13.   *Exactly! That costs real money!* 44

14.   *Right! That's right; this is the highest-priced product on the market!* 44

15.   *I can well understand that you see it that way.* 46

Create clarity 46

16.   *What exactly do you mean by "too expensive?"* 46

17.   *How much is "too expensive?"* 47

18.	Why?.. 47

19.	And where exactly is your top pain threshold
in terms of price? 47

20.	Too expensive? Compared with what?......................... 48

21.	And would/ will you not buy it because of that?................ 48

Bonus 4: "And would/ will you let the business fail
because of that?".. 49

22.	Other than the price, is there any point we need to clarify? 49

23.	Is it about buying cheap or low-priced for you? 49

Competitor comparison 50

24.	Can you please send me this offer? 50

25.	Would you be so kind as to email me the quote
so I can contrast the two for you? 50

26.	Who exactly offers this cheaper? 51

27.	What exactly are you offering? 51

28.	What are the differences with our offer?.................... 51

29.	And if you can buy it there why are you talking
with me about it? 51

30.	If they, the competitor, thought it was worth
more, they would be stupid not to charge
more for it, wouldn't they?.. 51

31.	And what if you had a problem with the product
and needed support?.. 52

32.	What do you think about comparing the offers
together (if necessary without competitor prices
and conditions), just to see where the differences
are and how I can get even more benefit for you?.............. 52

33.	A Mercedes costs more than a VW Golf. 52

Step by step 54

34.	Yes, gladly if you 54

35.   *What do I receive from you in return?*.................... 54

36.   *How much more would you lose for it?*................ 55

37.   *No problem! What do you want to leave out?*................ 55

Rationality, reason, and business administration 55

38.   *No problem! Then we'll just take the other, cheaper model!*.................... 55

39.   *Do you mean the price or the cost?*.................... 57

40.   *And how much do you save by using the product?*............ 57

41.   *By how much did you say your contribution margin will increase by using our process?*.......... 59

42.   *And how much time does that save you?*............ 59

43.   *And how much is the time you save worth to you?*............ 59

44.   *The question is, do you really want to go to the trouble of getting a few more quotes, spending hours studying and comparing them, only to end up saving maybe a few percent?*................ 59

45.   *That's why I have just the right financing offer for you*....... 60

46.   *One question: do you want to own it or use it?*.................. 60

47.   *How long do you plan to use the product, and how much will you invest per month?*.................. 62

Bonus 5: *This means we are talking about a difference of XY Euros.* 62

Create added value.................... 62

48.   *What else should (can) I add so the price-to-performance ratio is right for you?*.................... 63

49.   *We could, of course, talk about lowering the price, or we could work together to find ways to increase the value for you that will ultimately benefit you much more. What do you think?* 63

Bonus 6: *What if I add XY worth of Euros to your package for free; are we then in business?*.................... 64

Bonus 7: Other than a price reduction, which I must rule out, what else can I do to make the offer attractive enough for you to say yes? 64

Role change 64

50.   *Why is it still interesting for you?* 65

51.   *Why do you think so many of our customers buy it anyway?* 65

52.   *What would you have to give up if you chose something cheaper?* 65

53.   *You already know that I offer only the best quality, which has its price. So why did you come here?* 66

54.   *What have you already bought that you thought was too expensive and that you have now enjoyed for a long time?* 66

55.   *And what do you think I should do?* 66

56.   *Put yourself seriously in my position. They are now sitting opposite you as a customer, so to speak. What would you do in my place?* 67

57.   *Where exactly could we save some more to get an even better price for you?* 67

58.   *That's right! And how can I prove to you that it's worth every penny?* 67

Bonus 8: If you were to put yourself in my shoes and you couldn't offer a further discount, what would you do? 68

Emotion and human needs 68

59.   *Don't you deserve to treat yourself to something really good for once?* 68

60.   *And I always thought you were a decent person.* 69

61.   *However, your customers (members, children, employees, etc.) will be eternally grateful to you for this.* ... 69

62. *But in return, you are also one of the very first to have the opportunity to use this product.* 69

63. *You are right! The question is how much your safety is worth to you.* 70

64. *Right! The question is: How much is the safety of your family (employees, company, etc.) worth to you?* 70

65. *You don't have to buy it. You can continue to struggle with your old solution and the problems it causes. The choice is yours.* 70

66. *The product has its price, true. But your health is priceless.* 71

Recognition, honor, and ego 71

67. *Sorry! I thought you valued quality.* 71

68. *So, you don't want your spouse (children, employees, etc.) to have the best?* 71

69. *And how do you teach your spouse (children, employees, etc.) that you aren't giving them the best?* 72

70. *Can you not afford it? Or rather, can you afford it?* 72

71. *Sorry, I thought you had the appropriate financial resources.* 72

72. *You can then also tell everyone what a great product you have bought.* 73

73. *What do you think your neighbors (colleagues, customers, etc.) will say or think when they see you wearing it?* 73

74. *You'll probably get it for a lower price in a few months, but then you will no longer be the first.* 73

75. *Do you want to boast that you brought in a cheap consultant?* 74

Reverse logic 74

76. *That's exactly why you should buy it.* 75

77. *I made it that way especially for you.* 75

78.	I also have a guilty conscience about asking so much money from you, but that's nothing compared to the guilty conscience I would have if I offered you something cheaper.............................. 75

79.	Your money is currently yielding approx. 0% in the bank. These products increase in value by about 5% a year. So, the more money you put into these products and the less you have in the bank, the better for you. 77

80.	That's right. I want to save you the trouble you would have if you bought something cheap................. 77

81.	Can you afford to buy something cheap?........................... 77

Closing orientation.. 78

82.	I see! That means you'd rather have the cheaper one? 78

83.	Why would you still buy it?... 78

84.	Does that mean that if we agree on the price, I will get the order from you? 79

85.	What screw, apart from the price, can we turn to get you to say yes?.. 79

Bonus 9: Do you still want to buy/ have it? 79

Together to the goal 80

86.	What can we do together to convince your boss (your husband/ wife/ business partner, etc.)? 80

87.	And would you agree if it were your decision alone?.......... 80

88.	Then we should talk to the boss. When can we do that?.... 80

89.	We're in the same boat—my boss wouldn't agree to a lower price either. 81

90.	That's just as well. I have to go to the bathroom anyway. You are welcome to use my phone. 81

Body language.. 81

91.	Say nothing, pack up, and start walking 82

92. Shake head, look serious and sad and exhale audibly......... 82

Total openness.. 83

93. Disclose the calculation for the customer............................ 83

Argumentation... 83

94. I'm glad you said that! Let me tell you a short
story about this... 84

95. From my personal experience, the pain of separation
from the money we spend on high quality is
a short one. We enjoy the pleasure of the
great product for a lifetime, day after day.......................... 84

96. Yes, everything is getting more expensive.
The other day, I happened to have the ten-year-old
bill from my washing machine in my hands and
realized that I had paid twice as much for the new one. 84

97. In my experience, the more I invest in things that
I really like, the more satisfied I am with my
decision in the long run. 85

98. That's less than what you spend on XY each month. 85

Praise 86

99. Fortunately, you are someone who can distinguish
between "expensive" and "too expensive" very well.......... 86

100. Therefore, we sell only to people like you, who are also
willing to spend a little more money for the best quality.... 86

101. That's why I'm very glad that there are people
like you who can also afford something like this................. 86

Self-confident, cheeky, and impudent 87

102. Do you want a cheap supplier? I can gladly name
someone for you!.. 87

103. Absolutely right! If you want something cheap,
you are at the wrong address.. 87

104. Why do you waste your time and mine if you want
to buy something cheap? 88

105.   Do you want to buy a product or discount? 88

106.   And how much discount do you want? You can choose it. I will then calculate the appropriate price for you. 90

107.   Are you warm too? (If the customer says nothing but groans). 90

108.   I have calculated the prices, not estimated/ diced! 90

109.   That's a good one! I know a good one, too: A Rabbi and a Priest meet 92

110.   I am sorry, but I have nothing to give away. 92

111.   Oh, is it your birthday? I did not know that! 92

112.   Christmas has gone already, but now seriously 92

Bonus 10: I wonder if there's anything I can do about the price? Sure. For example, I could color the zeros in green and the eights in blue. That looks very good—at least that's what my customers say. 93

Bonus 11: Yes, there is always room for improvement................. 93

Quotes and sayings 93

113.   There will always be something cheaper. 95

114.   Do you know what EXPENSIVE stands for? Great, unique, incomparable, exquisite, and right for you............ 95

115.   Wilhelm Busch has already said, "On closer inspection, the price often also increases the respect!"...... 95

116.   You know how it is, what costs nothing is worth nothing... 96

117.   Quality never comes at a discount. 96

118.   If you buy cheap, you buy expensive. But you know that.... 96

The best objection-handling **97**

About the Author **99**

HOW YOU BENEFIT FROM THIS BOOK

Price talks and price negotiations are sometimes stressful, tense discussion situations for salespeople, but often also for the customer. After all, something is at stake for both, sometimes a great deal. Those who are better prepared for this situation can more easily and effectively assert their goals and get a bigger piece of the pie.

This book serves to prepare salespeople for dealing with customer price objections. And yes, even a customer who happens to get hold of this book could use it to prepare for the salesperson's arguments and approaches. May the better man win.

In this book, you will:

- ✓ find 118 possible answers to price objections of your customers

- ✓ learn how price objections might be disguised

- ✓ discover how to confidently take the wind out of your customers' sails when they ask for a discount

- ✓ learn the best psychological tips and tricks to refuting price arguments

- ✓ find humorous as well as very serious answers to price demands.

With this book, you will never be speechless in price discussions again.

Picture: Fotolia 129364556 S

NOTES ON THE THIRD, EXPANDED EDITION

The first editions of this book were very well received by salespeople and entrepreneurs of all kinds, but I also received a lot of feedback. I also had a couple of new ideas in the course of time, and some interesting new answers were sent in by readers.

I have therefore decided to integrate them into a new, completely revised edition that you now hold in your hands. I have also added further explanations and background information to the individual chapters or answers to "too expensive," making this book an even better little helper for your daily sales practice.

A few more have been added to the 118 answers to price objections, but I did not want to change the title for several reasons. Therefore, you will find the additional material listed as bonus answers in each chapter.

In the meantime, I have written other books on the topics of sales and especially price discussions, for which this book is the perfect supplement.

NEVER BE SPEECHLESS AGAIN

re you selling something? If so, you've probably heard this before and it may be bugging you. Price objections! These are common and strongly disliked by salespeople. In many industries today, there is hardly a sales call when a customer doesn't say "too expensive."

And many salespeople are still surprised by this and do not know what to say in response at the time or how to proceed with dealing with the objection.

However, as a salesperson, you can prepare and practice many ways of dealing with price objections. To make it easier for you to deal with "too expensive," you will find 118 variants (plus the new bonus answers) of handling objections in price discussions below.

This does not replace a well-thought-out price or negotiation strategy; rather, your objection-handling must be based on your price strategy. Also, these answers do not come close to covering the entire world of price negotiation.

However, the list of possible answers to "too expensive" helps you get to the heart of your strategy. This means you'll have the right answer to a customer's "too expensive" ready for all your sales talks, quickly and glibly, and you'll never be speechless in price discussions again.

"TOO EXPENSIVE" AND ITS RELATIVES

Your customer does not have to say, "too expensive." Rather, "too expensive" is representative of a series of similar objections. Price objections can be raised in a wide variety of formulations and disguises. For example, customers may say:

- *"It's too expensive."*

- *"It's too expensive for me!"*

- *"But that's already a lot!" or "But the price is already high!"*

- *"What else is going on price-wise?"*

- *"I'll offer you €1,200 for it!" or "I won't pay more than €1,200 for it!"*

- *"Five percent discount must still go there!" or "You must still accommodate me by 5%!"*

- *"But there you are (significantly) more expensive than the other offers I have!"*

- *"I've seen that a lot cheaper, though."*

- *"Your competitor is 5% lower!"*

- *"My boss (wife, husband, business partner, etc.) will never agree to that price!"*

- ➲ *"That is beyond my budget!"*

- ➲ *"I can't pay that much."*

- ➲ *"I don't want to pay that much."*

- ➲ *"It's not worth it to me."*

- ➲ *"I can't afford that."*

- ➲ *The customer says nothing at all but only exhales audibly or begins to groan.*

- ➲ *The customer tries to leave.*

EXPENSIVE OR TOO EXPENSIVE

A fundamental distinction must be made between a customer's "expensive" and "too expensive." Do they find the price for the offer reasonable but do not want to, or cannot, pay for such a purchase? Or do they consider the price for the service or product to be unreasonably high? Depending on the answer, you should proceed quite differently in dealing with the objection.

From this perspective, a price objection can occur in all price ranges from low to very high. By definition, "expensive" refers to something in a higher price range, but "too expensive" could be something that costs little in itself. For all basic situations, you will find suitable procedures or answers in the book.

THE OBJECTION-HANDLING MUST FIT THE PRICING STRATEGY

For all your customers' reactions to the mention of a price, you will find one or more variants of objection-handling being cheeky, polite, humorous, deadly serious, emotional, and rational. You will find responses to price objections that you can use only in very rare cases and those that will fit very often. Many variations are formulated for physical products but can usually be adapted just as well for services.

Ultimately, the right answer depends on your strategy as a salesperson, the reaction and person of the customer, the situation or business case, the relationship between you and your customer, and most importantly, yourself and your personality.

Not everything fits everyone and certainly not all the time. But the more options you have for dealing with price objections, the better your chances of achieving a higher price, a higher fee, and a better contribution margin.

Admittedly, some answer variants or strategies based on questions in the book are very "cheeky." These require not only a portion of courage to use but also very special situations in which they fit or are appropriate. This is what I've mostly observed with the individual variations, but even if that's not the case, you'll know which ones I'm talking about. You may never be able to apply these, but in a book that offers the most comprehensive collection of answers to "too expensive," they must be included. And even if a few seem downright exotic, there are definitely situations in which they are a reasonable response.

The best thing to do, therefore, is to read all the variants once and mark those (yes, you can write in this book) that fit you, your customers, and the objections and situations that occur most often in your practice.

If you always have a handful of such suitable responses and ways of reacting to price objections at the ready and, without having to think too much, can shake them out of your sleeve in a conversation, you have already achieved a great deal.

Picture: Fotolia 194590138 S

HOW TO SUCCESSFULLY HANDLE OBJECTIONS

Even if a price discussion or negotiation is a special situation during a sales process, price objections in the variants listed above are also just objections. Therefore, before we start with response variants to a "too expensive" from your customer, I would like to briefly explain the general procedure on how you can deal with objections of all kinds.

THE MOST COMMON MISTAKES WHEN DEALING WITH OBJECTIONS

It seems best to start with the most common mistakes:

- **Reaction at the touch of a button**
A basic mistake is that we often react too quickly, too impulsively, and too rashly to an objection. Your reaction can also come later, after a few breaths, or much later, like the next day or after a week; it depends entirely on the objection.

- **Do not let a customer finish**
A push-button response often means the salesperson doesn't even let their customer finish and cuts them off while they're still making their objection. This is not only impolite, but also valuable information can be missed.

- **Want to refute the objection**
  Most salespeople firmly assume that all objections must be rebutted. This is a false assumption. By no means must all objections be refuted or eliminated. How often have you bought something even though you had objections? You will find both approaches in the book, and yes, of course, there are objections that you must weaken, correct, or even eliminate, but it's by no means all.

- ***"Yes, but ..."***
  This is exactly the impulsive reaction that very often follows objections. "Yes, but ..." basically means, "That's not true, and I'll now tell you how it really is." This quickly leads to both interlocutors getting further entangled in their respective points of view with counterarguments. They thus cement their points of view increasingly firmly until, at some point, they can no longer get out of it, and agreement in any form becomes impossible.

- ***"But, in return, you also have/ get ..."***
  This variant to "Yes, but ...," or often in connection with it, "Yes, but for that you also have ..." is a salesperson's defense holding. They start to justify their price, and this weakens their position as a seller. If you justify the price, it means its position is weak, and you are too expensive.

- ***"You mustn't ..."***
  The customer can decide for themselves what they must and must not do. Often this statement is completed thus: "You are not allowed to compare our product with XY. That is something completely different." This may be true, but it would be fundamentally wrong to tell the customer

that in this way. That is paternalism, and many customers will rightly resist this stance.

- **"You must ..."**
  This statement is like the previous one. It also causes many interlocutors to resist, with "must" having an even stronger effect than "must not."

- **"I've never heard anything like that before."**
  This is also very common. Not only, but especially in the case of complaints, sentences like this are often heard. The customer raises an objection that, from their point of view, makes sense and is justified. With this statement, the seller makes them understand that they are the only one who sees it that way and that it is, therefore, a wrong or "nonsense" view. This approach is also not conducive to creating a good basis for a successful sales transaction.

HANDLING OBJECTIONS - HOW IT WORKS

Now that we have highlighted what not to do in the event of a customer objection, the question is how to proceed. Basically, the more successful approach is the one that is the opposite of the listed errors. In concrete terms, this means taking the below steps and doing so in the order given.

1. **Relaxed basic attitude**
   A relaxed basic attitude, which is generally highly recommended during a sales talk, is also very helpful when dealing with objections. It takes the pressure out of a situation. You don't have to react immediately; rather, allow yourself more time, so the impulse to refute the objection

is not there. And you certainly don't have to defend yourself from this position. Keep breathing calmly and maintain eye contact. "Look smart and keep breathing," is how one of my teachers used to put it very pointedly.

2. Listen and hear out

Under pressure to respond immediately and refute an objection, salespeople often fall over their customers' words. Just listen, really listen, and wait patiently and attentively until the customer has said everything they want to say. While doing this, maintain eye contact and, if appropriate, ask feedback questions such as, "So that means, if I understand you correctly, that you mean...?" Nod and make sounds of agreement (uh-huh), which does not mean you agree with the content; rather, you are demonstrating that you are really listening and sincerely trying to understand. This makes the customer feel taken seriously and appreciated. This is an enormously important basis for further handling of an objection, especially a price objection.

3. Express thanks and appreciation

This step will usually combine with step two, which is absolutely fine. Why should you thank the customer for objecting, even a price objection? It's a fair question and an understandable one at this point. Imagine if your customer doesn't voice their objection but still has it in mind. Instead, they bring up some excuse (á la "I'll think about it again"), leave, and are never seen again.

Which do you prefer? If your customer voices their objection, they are doing you a favor. After all, you can then respond and do something about it; it's an opportunity. "Thank you for being so open about this. I really appreciate it." You might express your appreciation in this way or with something similar.

4. Question the objection

Objections, including price objections, are often very unclear, general, and not very specific. "Too expensive," "What else is possible?" or "But I've already been offered this cheaper" are far from sufficient as bases for any meaningful response. Therefore, in a next step, question the customer's statement.

"What exactly do you mean by 'too expensive?'" For example, this is how this question could be phrased. The "What exactly do you mean by XY?" question will be a good fit for many objections. When your customer responds, it will often be necessary to question further. "What else?" or "How exactly am I supposed to understand this?" might be such follow-up questions. Do not be satisfied until you think you have really understood what your customer is saying or wants.

Quite apart from the information you gain from their answers, you gain time to think about next steps while they are answering, without appearing inattentive, of course. More significantly, you keep the lead in the conversation because "They who ask, leads."

5. Resolve the objection

Resolving a price objection will not always be possible and sometimes not even necessary. But, if it is, then it is appropriate at this point at the earliest. Before that, you simply know too little, and your customer still feels they are not fully understood or taken seriously.

This basic approach to dealing with objections will, as you will see, not be compatible with all 118+ responses in this book. Nevertheless, it is important to know them and, regardless of the below procedures and variants, use them repeatedly. Combine them as you see fit with the strategy of your choice.

But now to the 118+ answers to price objections that the book title promises.

118 VARIANTS OF HANDLING OBJECTIONS OF "TOO EXPENSIVE"

To make it easier to find certain types of objection handling, the 118+ variants are divided into categories. Some answers would fit several categories.

Often, two or more of the variants can also be combined in the course of the price discussion or even in one sentence.

REJECTION AND WITHDRAWAL

These variants of objection-handling are suitable for showing very clearly that it is "over" here and now. You can either use them at the beginning of a price discussion to make it clear there is no room for negotiation or in the course of the price negotiation when you can or no longer want to go any further. You must, therefore, also be prepared not to make the deal. True to the motto, "Better no deal than one where you lose money."

By the way, this is something that applies to price negotiations in general. If you want to be in a strong position in a negotiation, you must be prepared to leave the negotiation without a result or with a "no" from the customer. If you are not, you are in a weak position from the start. If the customer knows this, you have little chance of ending the price negotiation halfway successfully and achieving healthy margins and contribution margins.

1. *That's a pity; I thought we were going to do business.*

This variant is most effective if you combine it with a body language statement (No. 91 or No. 92) and attempt to leave. The customer must realize you mean business. Lean back demonstratively, slam your documents shut, start packing up, and, if necessary, start to leave.

2. *We can talk about everything but the price!*

You can use this variant right at the beginning of a conversation before your customer even raises a price objection. This makes it clear from the start that you are not willing to negotiate on price. Above all, customers who "would have tried," i.e., customers with weak price objections trying to get a better price will be dissuaded if you show strength in this way right from the start.

3. *No! You can't because ...*

Saying "No" is very hard for us to do for several reasons, and at the same time it's one of the most significant and profitable skills in business. We don't want to seem unsympathetic; our relationship with our customer is hopefully a very good one and we don't want to jeopardize it. The customer may have already done us a favor or it's the end of the month and we still desperately need sales. These are probably the most common reasons for our aversion to the word "No."

However, you can significantly increase your customer's acceptance of "No" with a little communicative, psychological trick. By the way, this will also make it a little easier for you to say "No." Add a reason to the "No" that you introduce with "because." Studies have shown that "No, because ..." significantly increases customer acceptance. By the way, this also applies to situations where you have fulfilled requests or want to enforce demands. The justification does not have to be particularly creative. A halfway plausible, "No, because we have already calculated extremely tightly," or "No, because raw material prices have risen sharply," is also sufficient.

"No, because ..." is also something you can say several times in a row. It is then called the "no-egg." However, it is best to introduce it with a sentence of understanding and change your words a little, so it does not sound too monotonous. For example, customer: "can you do something more with the price there?" Salesperson: "I can well understand that you are watching your budget. However, I can't do anything more about the price because ..."

Picture: Canva

Bonus 1: I'll tell you right up front, you won't want me.

This form of anticipatory treatment of price objections can be successfully applied to high-priced items or, as in this case, services. An American colleague, John, shared how he applies it during a seminar.

A potential customer, a high-level executive, comes forward in response to a referral. "We have bought a company and want to merge the sales organizations, and you've been recommended to me as an expert to do that." John: "I'm very pleased, but you won't want me." Customer (irritated): "Why wouldn't I want you?" John: "I'm very expensive. I charge $XY per day and I know from experience that's why many clients don't book me."

The client now has two choices. They could say, "You're right, John. In that case, I'll pass." Of course, that would be an indictment of a high-level executive of a larger company. Or they could say, "John, you can take it from me that we certainly have the resources for professional consulting." In this way, price objections are out of the way from the start.

Too American? Wouldn't work in Europe? Think of the Crisan commercial (an anti-dandruff shampoo) in the 70s and 80s proudly proclaiming, "Crisan is expensive as hell, but it works." In slightly modified form, you can most certainly tell your customer at the beginning of the conversation, "Right up front we're probably talking about a significant investment in the €25,000 range."

EVASION

Evading or even ignoring a price objection is a method of objection-handling that can be used well, especially in cases where the objection is weak or when you notice the customer is "just asking" but not demanding. In this case, the variants of the previous category (refusal and withdrawal) can also be used very well.

If the issue of "lower price" is truly significant to the customer, the objection will come back. If not, why bother with a price objection at all?

4. Ignore and do not react at all

The hardest way to dodge the issue is to just keep talking as if nothing had happened. It works particularly well with price objections in statement form ("But that's already expensive!") but it is more challenging to use with objections in question form, like, "How much discount can you give me there?" This approach could be perceived as very impolite.

5. I see, so you find the price is higher than expected. Can I ask you a question? What do you think about the build quality?

This variant is the much more elegant way of dealing with objections by dodging. However, it consists of several parts.

In the first part, you repeat the customer's statement, if necessary, slightly modified by reframing. You will learn what reframing is and how to use it successfully in the next section. Thus, you express that you understand the customer. However, this does not mean that you agree with them.

After that, ask if you can ask them a question. The customer will always answer "yes" to this question.

In the second part, you then ask a question about an element you know the customer particularly appreciates about your offer, for example, the quality of workmanship, the flexibility, or the durability, something the customer expects to get a lot of value from but that has nothing directly to do with the price and diverts from the price objection.

Once the customer has responded, you can ask more questions to get even further away from the issue of price.

Bonus 2: Oh, one more thing just came to mind. Is the tire dimension right for you?

However, you can also directly ask a question that sounds as if it had just occurred to you. Since your mind was occupied with this question, you missed the price objection. At least, that's the impression the customer will get.

If the customer does bring up their price objection again after one of these variations of your response, then continue with another appropriate method from this book.

REFRAMING OR REINTERPRETATION

Reframing or reinterpretation is a communication strategy that can be used not only in dealing with objections but also in many other situations. A distinction can be made between meaning reframing and context reframing.

In meaning reframing, which can be used very well in objection handling, different meanings are attributed to the customer's words or actions. For example, the price objection itself means that the customer wants to buy. If the customer had no interest in buying at all, then they probably wouldn't even bother bringing up a price objection.

Meaning reframing also involves replacing the customer's words with other, more positive (or sometimes deliberately negative) ones. "Expensive" becomes "valuable" or "high-priced," a "price objection" becomes "feedback," and a "rejection" becomes a "not-yet-agreement."

Context reframing can also be used in objection handling. Here, one and the same action is evaluated quite differently in different contexts/situations. For example, in terms of meeting budgets, it may be bad to buy something high-priced. But when it comes to showing one's social environment what one can afford, the price of a product often cannot be high enough.

6. ***So you think the price is still not quite what you want.***

> Suppose the customer said, "That product is too expensive for me." There are several words in this response that refrain. "Still" means "it will get there," "not quite" means

"but a little," and "meet the expectations" is less bad than "too expensive."

7. Did you want something CHEAPER?

Here, the customer's desire for a price reduction is reinterpreted negatively. You can reinforce this by emphasizing the word "cheaper" while slightly contorting your face and shaking your head ever so slightly as if it were something unpleasant, even repulsive. A lower price is what many want, but something "cheap" is what no one wants. Customers want to buy valuable products and services.

8. The fact that you ask me for a lower price means that you want it. Do I see that right?

This type of objection handling through reframing turns the price objection, which is often seen as negative, into something positive. The customer is led to believe that the price objection is an expression of their desire to buy. This variant increases the pressure to close the deal (see also the category "Closing orientation").

9. Right! It is a valuable product!

Saying "true" after your customer declares, "That's a lot you're asking!" makes it hard for them to disagree with your statement. The expression "valuable" used in place of their "expensive" has a positive connotation. After that, don't say anything else; just look at the customer and move on in the process. You can also support this verbally by saying something like, "Well, now that we've discussed that, the only question left is ..." A bit cheeky? Yes. But cheekiness wins out, as we all know.

Picture: Shutterstock

10. *Thank you for your feedback. So that means you still need more information to properly assess the value for you?*

Here, the customer's objection as such is transformed into "feedback," thus turning something negative or critical back into something positive. This statement also focuses the customer away from the price towards the value. It is not about lowering the price; this is virtually excluded as an option, but increasing the value, which is already there in the customer's mind.

11. *That means it is only about 100 € more than you originally wanted to spend.*

Here, the reframing lies in the structure of the observation. Instead of the total price, the focus here is on the price difference. This amount is naturally significantly lower and therefore easier to absorb. The reframing is further supported by the "only," thus, "expensive" becomes "not so bad."

Bonus 3: It all depends on what is important to you and what you are trying to achieve. Many of my clients choose it BECAUSE it looks and is expensive, and that's a deciding factor in how it looks to the outside world.

In this context, reframing the customer understands there are situations and purposes of your product in which it is important that it is expensive and works. The apparent disadvantage thus becomes a weighty advantage.

AGREE

The below variants of objection-handling can be used with great success when the customer remarks that the price is very high but does not say "too expensive." After all, just because they think the price is high or something is expensive doesn't mean they won't buy it! How many times have you bought something where the price made you sweat or was significantly higher than what you had planned to spend? So why argue and not just say, "YES, that's so!"

12. *True. As is so often the case, quality has its price.*

In this objection treatment, consent is used to emphasize the quality of the offer by using a high price as proof of high quality. This connection between quality and price is firmly anchored in all of us and works in this direction. We often infer a correspondingly high quality from a high price, especially when we don't buy something often.

13. *Exactly! That costs real money!*

Why make a secret of the price? High prices are sometimes something to be proud of as a seller. Sometimes there is even a slight reframing in the opposite direction. The customer says, "a bit much" and the salesperson turns it into "a great deal."

14. *Right! That's right; this is the highest-priced product on the market!*

This objection treatment is the logical continuation of No. 13. The price itself is the quality criterion. This means that for some products or services, quality increases in the eyes of the customer as prices rise. This effect is called reverse price elasticity.

Picture: Shutterstock

15. *I can well understand that you see it that way.*

No arguments, no reframing, simply understanding, but, strictly speaking, not agreeing. You can understand a point of view, but you do not have to agree with it. Therefore, this variant of objection-handling is also applicable to contrary views. Often, this alone is enough. Customers sometimes don't want a solution at all but just some understanding of their situation.

CREATE CLARITY

In many cases, price objections are very diffuse and unclear. "Too expensive," for example, involves a comparison (the "too"). But what is the customer comparing it with? Their budget, their last purchase, what they thought it would cost, or what their partner or boss said was the upper limit? You often don't know. That's why it's important to get clarity before you move forward with the price conversation, and you get clarity primarily by asking questions.

16. *What exactly do you mean by "too expensive?"*

This question can cause slight confusion for the customer. They do not know exactly what you mean and start to explain their point of view. Sometimes, this question produces entirely new insights for the salesperson. If the customer says, "too expensive," you can almost always use this question as a first approach. After the additional insights you gain from the answers, you can then decide how to proceed.

17. *How much is "too expensive?"*

If the customer tells you their asking price or the difference between the asking price and their price, you have an advantage. Often a seller will make a mistake here in the price negotiations and say first how much they would be willing to concede. At the same time, however, it is fair to say that their answer may not be the truth. They may state a much lower target price than they hope to get from you. As a result, they set a low-price anchor from which you, the seller, must now move the price up.

18. *Why?*

A simple "Why?" combined with an absolutely amazed and slightly concerned look can be very disarming. It leaves a lot of room for all sorts of answers from the customer, which in turn can bring more clarity and insight to their perspective for you. It's a response that the customer isn't expecting from you here, which can throw them off and confuse them a bit. And confusion of this kind can sometimes be beneficial in price discussions.

In this way, you turn the argumentation pressure around. It is no longer you as the salesperson who must present arguments that justify the price; now, the customer must explain their demand for a price reduction and justify it to you. This is a much more satisfactory situation for the salesperson.

19. *And where exactly is your top pain threshold in terms of price?*

This variant of objection-handling is like No. 17, except that it prompts the customer to go further and reveal their real limit rather than just their desired price or idea. You can ask this question after they have revealed their asking price. By doing so, you indirectly imply the price or discount they gave you is not their true limit. Even if this may seem a bit strange, it may well be that your customer will increase their desired price or soften their demand in response to this question.

20. *Too expensive? Compared with what?*

As mentioned at the beginning of the chapter, it is important for you as a salesperson to know what your customer is comparing with what when they say, "too expensive." You can then choose your strategy accordingly. It makes a massive difference for your ongoing approach whether your customer compares with their self-imposed budget, with what their partner thought it would cost, with a competitor's product, which may not be comparable at all, or with what they paid three years ago when they last bought the product.

21. *And would/ will you not buy it because of that?*

Counterattack is often the best defense. Instead of trying to mitigate the price objection, simply ask the customer here if it is so significant that they would or will not buy because of it. If the objection is rather weak, your customer will counter and say something like, "Not that, I like your offer, yes. I just wanted ..." and then your negotiating position is strengthened. If they say the word, "Yes," at least you know they are serious.

Bonus 4: "And would/ will you let the business fail because of that?"

With this slightly tightened variant to the previous one, you virtually blame the customer for the failure and put the burden on their shoulders.

22. Other than the price, is there any point we need to clarify?

This variant of objection-handling is extremely important. The price of your offer should be the last thing you discuss. It only makes sense when it is clear exactly what the customer wants and in what form. Therefore, all other ambiguities must be removed before any price discussion.

This will also prevent the customer from pursuing salami tactics where after they have agreed on a price they move on to payment terms and then onto delivery and so on. Some professional negotiators and buyers have seven, eight or even more issues to negotiate on. With this approach, you "force" your counterpart to put all their cards on the table.

23. Is it about buying cheap or low-priced for you?

"Cheap" and "favorable" are not the same thing. "Cheap" refers to the absolute amount, while "inexpensive" expresses a relativity, a comparison. Something can be very expensive, but still be cheap. This subtle difference in relation to your customer creates clarity for your negotiation strategy and further approach in the sales conversation.

COMPETITOR COMPARISON

Price objections often come in the form of a competitor comparison. This involves mentioning an (alleged) competitor's offer that is a lot cheaper. Even if this is the case, it is important to ensure that apples are compared with apples. Again, the goal is to create more clarity, so work often with questions instead of statements or arguments to handle objections.

24. Can you please send me this offer?

Not every customer will, but you can ask. The best way to do this is to make the question sound casual. You increase the likelihood of getting the competitive offer if you still combine the question with an explanation. Introduce this explanation with "because." This, as mentioned earlier, increases the likelihood of your customer's agreement. "Because this is the best way for us to compare the two offers!" But be careful! Proceed with tact. You don't want to imply that the customer can't do it themselves.

25. Would you be so kind as to email me the quote so I can contrast the two for you?

This type of objection-handling is an extension of the previous one. You formulate a question but intonate your desire for the competitor's offer as a "command," albeit a very nice one. You do this by lowering your voice at the end of that sentence. Unconsciously, this is associated with a command. Deliver it in such a way that it sounds casual as if you are asking for a small thing, a common procedure, a matter of course.

26. **_Who exactly offers this cheaper?_**

This question should come up in your price discussion, especially if the customer remains very general and unspecific in their mention of the competitor's offer.

27. **_What exactly are you offering?_**

Apples are often compared with oranges. This question attempts to bring clarity to the comparison.

28. **_What are the differences with our offer?_**

This question contains a presupposition, namely that there are differences. At the same time, it is left to the customer to name them. It is much more convincing if they come up with them themself.

29. **_And if you can buy it there why are you talking with me about it?_**

This (somewhat cheeky) question rightly insinuates that the customer is interested in buying from you even though a competitor is cheaper. Would they talk to you otherwise? The reasoning is again left to the customer.

30. **_If they, the competitor, thought it was worth more, they would be stupid not to charge more for it, wouldn't they?_**

Thus, you conclude from the competitor's lower price that they do not believe their product is worth more, which also does not seem logical. In this way, you question the quality of the competitor's offer without attacking it directly. It's a very elegant way of dealing with objections.

31.   *And what if you had a problem with the product and needed support?*

Painting the devil on the wall is a widespread, general variant of objection-handling or conversation management in sales (e.g., classically in insurance). This question will work particularly well if, in addition to the price, security is a significant purchase motive for the customer and the competitor cannot offer this security, perhaps because it is located abroad or is only an online shop.

32.   *What do you think about comparing the offers together (if necessary without competitor prices and conditions), just to see where the differences are and how I can get even more benefit for you?*

You side with the customer to achieve the best for them. Can they object to that?

33.   *A Mercedes costs more than a VW Golf.*

A confident statement that, of course, implicitly assumes that your offer is the Mercedes and the competitor's offer is the Golf. In the automotive industry, this variant of objection-handling must be adapted accordingly.

Picture: Shutterstock

STEP BY STEP

If we receive something, we must give something back! This is a fundamental principle of human interaction. It is almost a compulsion that we find very difficult to escape, or can you manage not to give back to someone who gives you a Christmas present? This principle is based on the psychological mechanism of reciprocity.

Therefore, it is only natural and logical to ask what the customer would give you if you gave them a better price. "Move for move" is the motto. After all, if you were to give a better price without getting anything in return, how respectable would your original price have been?

34. *Yes, gladly if you ...*

Instead of going into resistance, you simply make a counterclaim with this objection treatment, in the spirit of move for move.

35. *What do I receive from you in return?*

This version is like the previous one, except you leave it up to the customer to decide what consideration to give. Maybe it's one you haven't thought of yet or more than you would have dared to ask for. This question again contains a pre-assumption (presupposition), namely that you will receive something in any case; the question is only "what?" For this question to work well, you must ask it with a certain implication that you will get something back.

36. *How much more would you lose for it?*

This question is used to target the consideration to a larger purchase quantity, which can make sense in many cases. This is the classic volume discount

37. *No problem! What do you want to leave out?*

Isn't that the most natural thought for price negotiations ever? If your customer wants to, or can only, pay less, they will naturally receive less service from you. After all, it would be more than strange and not a serious scenario if the customer, just because they asked, suddenly paid significantly less for the same thing apart from some small concession to a good customer relationship. It is important that this type of objection to "too expensive" is also delivered in body language and voice as if this approach were the most natural in the world.

RATIONALITY, REASON, AND BUSINESS ADMINISTRATION

Far from all slogans and communicative feints, rationality and business considerations can be used very well for dealing with objections in many cases. Especially where it is a matter of savings or gains that the customer has through your offer, it makes a lot of sense to use such arguments.

38. *No problem! Then we'll just take the other, cheaper model!*

This answer to "too expensive" is a variant of the previous one. It is particularly suitable when a product is available in different price ranges or when you can increase or decrease the value or price of the offer relatively easily by adding or omitting features or services.

Picture: Shutterstock

39. *Do you mean the price or the cost?*

When asked this question, your customer will often be irritated and ask, "What do you mean?" Then you can explain the difference. The price is what they pay right away or even later; the cost, on the other hand, can far exceed the price, especially when calculated over the life of a product. A product may have additional costs over its useful life, or it may have savings that need to be factored into the cost calculation. With cars, this comparison of costs is often made (fuel consumption, insurance, etc.). These are then calculated down to the kilometers driven.

This variant of objection-handling can also be used very well when the customer compares your offer with their previous solution or another alternative. This may be lower in price than your offer, but much more expensive when comparing costs. If this approach is a good fit for you because your prices are high but the unit costs (km, time units, number of uses, etc.) are very competitive, then you could even use it as a sales strategy in a very basic way and communicate these costs instead of prices from the beginning.

40. *And how much do you save by using the product?*

By using products or services, the customer may be saving time, money, resources, etc. This objection follows from the previous one. The point is to show that price alone is often not a suitable evaluation criterion for a purchase decision. And if the customer themselves state how much they will save, and not you, so much the better. You should use this approach especially if you are sure your customer will actually save money when using your offer.

Picture: Shutterstock

41. By how much did you say your contribution margin will increase by using our process?

Not only savings, as in the previous variant, can be quoted in the price negotiation but also additional contribution margins or income of some kind. This may shift the cost comparison back in your favor because you can offset the income against the costs.

42. And how much time does that save you?

This response to the customer's objection specifically points to the time saved and is a variant of No. 40. Which of these variants you use also depends on what is particularly important to the customer—their costs, their time (No. 43), the yield, the security, or even simplicity and the absence of problems. You can thus directly address all potential human needs and use them for objection-handling.

43. And how much is the time you save worth to you?

Many people don't even know how much their time is worth. With this question, you encourage the customer to think about it. In many cases, the calculation results in a great argument in favor of your offer.

44. The question is, do you really want to go to the trouble of getting a few more quotes, spending hours studying and comparing them, only to end up saving maybe a few percent?

Haven't you often experienced how tedious it can be to obtain and compare offers and how relieved you are when you have then made the - hopefully correct - decision? With this type of objection handling, you give the customer the chance to save themselves this effort and shorten the decision path. If, as in the previous variant, they have calculated the value of their time, the further detailed comparison of offers does not pay off for them either.

45. *That's why I have just the right financing offer for you.*

Too expensive? No problem! What is financing for? Customers finance almost everything today from steam irons to industrial equipment. Financing, in the form of leasing, credit, etc., has many advantages for you as a seller but also for the customer. First, it eliminates or at least reduces the pain of having to spend a large sum of money straight away.

Second, your offer becomes affordable for the customer, even though they do not currently have the funds for it. Third, the amounts, e.g., in the case of car leasing, often sound very small when broken down into months, and last but not least, you can improve your contribution margin by means of financing through commissions from the financing institution. For the customer, the smaller monthly amounts not only make the expenses easier to bear but also easier to plan.

46. *One question: do you want to own it or use it?*

A very pointed version of the financing question, which is aimed at the fact that with leasing, you are not the owner, but you still get the benefit of full use. This objection handling question will irritate many customers and they will ask, "What do you mean?" And you're off the objection and discussing a solution option. Also, funding makes it harder to compare prices because many factors would need to be compared. And less comparability is good for you if your offer is not the cheapest (but may be the cheapest).

Picture: Shutterstock

47. *How long do you plan to use the product, and how much will you invest per month?*

With this way of responding to a customer objection in the price negotiation, you steer the customer's thoughts away from the absolute price and break it down to a less painful monthly consideration. Again, if the customer figures it out for themselves, it's more convincing. Encourage self-awareness in your customers wherever possible, especially in price discussions.

Bonus 5: *This means we are talking about a difference of XY Euros.*

With this approach, the focus is shifted away from the total price to the difference with a comparable price. This can be a competitor's offer, the customer's budget, or even a second, more expensive offer variant from you that the customer could consider. The advantage here is that this amount is much smaller than the total price. You can also combine this strategy with No. 47 and break down the difference to the duration of use (years, months, or even days depending on the product or service) or even to the expected number of uses. This usually makes the amount at stake very small very quickly and sounds easier to get over.

CREATE ADDED VALUE

Customers buy when they think the value they will receive exceeds the price they will pay. And if it still doesn't, there are two ways to handle that objection. Lower the price or increase the value.

Most customers, like sellers, usually prefer to only think about lowering the price. But why not increase the value? E.g., by adding an extra or extra performance? For you as a seller, this has the advantage that the additional costs are often far lower than the increase in value or the additional benefit for the customer.

48. ***What else should (can) I add so the price-to-performance ratio is right for you?***

By asking this question, you assume that your customer is open to an additional service instead of a price reduction. The advantage of asking the customer to add something is that they may have an idea for added value that you may not have thought of. The disadvantage is that the customer might ask for something more that you can't or won't add for free. In that case, you would have to reject the proposal.

49. ***We could, of course, talk about lowering the price, or we could work together to find ways to increase the value for you that will ultimately benefit you much more. What do you think?***

This is a much gentler variant than the previous one of dissuading the customer from the idea of reducing the price in favor of additional performance. Its disadvantage is that the customer could, and often will, immediately opt for the price reduction again. However, you could also make them so curious that they want to know how you propose to increase the price. This approach is certainly worth a try.

Bonus 6: What if I add XY worth of Euros to your package for free; are we then in business?

With this version, you make a proposal for a value increase instead of asking the customer, as in strategy No. 48. This way, you naturally only propose something that is also okay for you from a costing point of view, and you thus have more control than in No. 48 on this point. If you have made a clean needs assessment, then you also know what is particularly interesting for the customer.

Bonus 7: Other than a price reduction, which I must rule out, what else can I do to make the offer attractive enough for you to say yes?

If you proceed in this way, you exclude variants of the value increase that are unfavorable or simply not feasible for you. In this way, however, you can exclude not only a price reduction but also, in principle, everything else that is not okay for you.

ROLE CHANGE

As a salesperson, you can make objection-handling much easier in many cases by reversing the roles and letting the customer do the selling themselves. Let them slip into your role. Questions are a very good tool for this. Let your customer convince themselves that your offer is the best for them. Their arguments are much more credible and therefore more effective than yours. For you as a salesperson, this means asking the right questions, sitting back, and letting your customer do the selling.

50. ***Why is it still interesting for you?***

In this type of objection-handling, you again work with a presupposition (pre-assumption) by assuming that your offer is interesting for your customer. When they respond they not only agree with you but also provide the arguments themselves. Making this pre-assumption is absolutely justified in many cases and sales situations. For example, if you have a second or third meeting with the customer to talk about their possible purchase it is clear they are basically interested. Otherwise, they would not talk to you again.

51. ***Why do you think so many of our customers buy it anyway?***

This question again packs a very elegant presupposition: "so many." If your customer answers this, then it is tacitly accepted that it is "many" who nevertheless buy. There is no more talk about that, only about "why." This question, as well as some of the others in this section, will get the customer thinking. They usually won't have an answer ready right away. That's fine and perfectly okay. Give them the time and, after they have given one or more answers, ask "and why else?" once or even more times.

52. ***What would you have to give up if you chose something cheaper?***

And here follows the next question with a presupposition. This time it is assumed that "cheaper" is synonymous with "doing without." Your customer will tell you what they must do without but perhaps don't want to. In this way, you cause your customer to compare apples with apples and exclude the pears and other fruit from consideration.

53. *You already know that I offer only the best quality, which has its price. So why did you come here?*

A somewhat bolder way of dealing with objections that requires a certain amount of self-confidence on the part of the seller. It is an invitation to speak plainly and at the same time it is made clear, once again, that you offer the best quality. As mentioned briefly earlier, the customer is not just sitting with you for fun and investing time in sales talks or price negotiations, and if they do, they have reasons to do so which you, of course, want to know.

54. *What have you already bought that you thought was too expensive and that you have now enjoyed for a long time?*

Buying something that was over our budget but that we've had a lot of fun with ever since—haven't we all experienced that? Your customer most likely has, too. With this question, you steer your interlocutor away from the high price and towards the long-lasting good feeling that remains even after the pain of spending money is long gone.

55. *And what do you think I should do?*

When you use this type of objection-handling in a price discussion, make it clear that you are really interested in your customer's opinion. In this way, you let them slip into the role of advisor. Be surprised at what ideas may come from their side, ideas that sometimes you would never have considered.

Of course, the answer to such a question could also be unfeasible suggestions or something not helpful to you. In this case, you can use the variant I describe in Bonus 7 in the next step or link it to No. 55 (see Bonus 8).

56. _Put yourself seriously in my position. They are now sitting opposite you as a customer, so to speak. What would you do in my place?_

This is a slightly modified version of the previous approach. By asking questions in this way, you increase the likelihood that they will really put themselves in your shoes and think less about solutions in their favor, rather supplying answers that represent a course of action you can both live well with.

57. _Where exactly could we save some more to get an even better price for you?_

Again, you are addressing your customer as a consultant. Leaving something out is often a good way to reduce the price. Many products and services have elements that customers would gladly do without in favor of a lower price. And who knows better than the customer themselves what they can do without. After all, they know their needs and requirements best of all.

58. _That's right! And how can I prove to you that it's worth every penny?_

A confident statement coupled with a question that includes the presupposition that your offer is worth every penny. It's all about the "how to prove it." Again, let your customer provide the arguments.

> **Bonus 8: If you were to put yourself in my shoes and you couldn't offer a further discount, what would you do?**

This is the linkage of the idea described in Bonus 7 with No. 55. You put the customer in your position and at the same time exclude variants that are not desired or not possible.

Generally, questions are one of the most effective and therefore most significant tools in dealing with price objections as well as those involving other issues. In fact, I would argue that the ability to ask good questions is an important skill for a successful salesperson.

EMOTION AND HUMAN NEEDS

Humans have a whole range of needs beyond basic physiological needs such as eating, drinking, sleeping, etc., including safety, health, and connection with others. You can make good use of these needs in objection-handling, especially if you know which needs are particularly important to your customer. How do you find that out? By asking the right questions. One that is particularly appropriate for this is, "What is important to you when you are thinking about buying XY?"

Below you will find different variants of objection-handling that fit various needs.

> **59. Don't you deserve to treat yourself to something really good for once?**

Rewarding yourself is important. Your customer works hard, too. With this rhetorical question you reframe your product as a "reward" and point out to them that it's time for another one.

60. *And I always thought you were a decent person.*

You can use this variant of the objection in two ways, either humorously or seriously. In the case of the humorous variant, it must be clear from the way you pronounce the sentence that you are not entirely serious, but it does have a serious core. In this way, you are saying, "I can still laugh about it, but that's it!" In the serious variant your sincere indignation must be clearly expressed. Your customer does not want to appear "indecent" and may begin to soften their statement.

61. *However, your customers (members, children, employees, etc.) will be eternally grateful to you for this.*

Many people are strongly motivated by doing good to others. It is precisely with those that this variant of objection handling will fall on fertile ground in the sales conversation, even if your customer does not realize it.

62. *But in return, you are also one of the very first to have the opportunity to use this product.*

This motivator, being the first and holding a pioneering role, is also widespread. This buying motive ensures, for example, that long lines of people always form when Apple launches a new iPhone. Of course, you can buy the product a few days or even weeks later, relaxed and without queuing, in the store or online. But being first is important for many customers.

63.   *You are right! The question is how much your safety is worth to you.*

With this question you grab your conversation partner with a basic need that everyone has in one form or another and that's security. We are constantly paying for security in some form, sometimes directly, for example, by buying insurance, and sometimes indirectly, for example, when we choose the product of a well-known brand, trusting it is the safer choice. Given the right offer, security is, of course, always worth more than the price they pay for your product.

64.   *Right! The question is: How much is the safety of your family (employees, company, etc.) worth to you?*

This variant of objection-handling goes one step further and couples the need for security with the need to do something good for others. Whenever security is involved, there is naturally a little fear of not having it or losing it. This fear tends to be amplified by involving others, if that fits your offering, in this way.

65.   *You don't have to buy it. You can continue to struggle with your old solution and the problems it causes. The choice is yours.*

The motive addressed by this statement is "simplicity and freedom from problems." And it's true; they really don't have to buy it, they just have to suffer the consequences. This kind of objection-handling can be disarming and is especially useful when it is not primarily about comparison with competitor offers but rather about using a solution or product at all.

66. *The product has its price, true. But your health is priceless.*

People generally place too low a value on health. Only when it is no longer present does it become enormously important. This statement (which can alternatively be formulated as a question as in No. 64) draws your customer's attention to this fact.

RECOGNITION, HONOR, AND EGO

The need for recognition is such a widespread and significant one that I have grouped variants of objection handling specifically suited to it into a category of their own. Some of them are brash and full-bodied but quite applicable in some situations. Depending on the situation, the interlocutor, and the need, you can also soften harsh statements and questions with a wink.

67. *Sorry! I thought you valued quality.*

In saying so, you imply that your customer does not do this. In many cases, they will contradict you, especially if you hit a nerve. At the same time, you are packaging a presupposition in these variants, namely that your offer stands for quality. However, we will not discuss this any further at this point.

68. *So, you don't want your spouse (children, employees, etc.) to have the best?*

This, of course, is a very harsh formulation that you should or can use only in very special situations. Your customer is almost forced to answer this question with "of course I want that." In doing so, they play into the hands of your argument and tacitly agree with the hidden statement that your offer is the best.

69. ***And how do you teach your spouse (children, employees, etc.) that you aren't giving them the best?***

The same applies as in the previous variant; it's a very harsh formulation that you can only use if you know exactly what you are doing. Again, you will find a hidden presupposition; they don't begrudge their loved ones the best.

70. ***Can you not afford it? Or rather, can you afford it?***

This question grabs many people very deeply at the roots of ego and honor. Admitting that you can't afford something is very difficult for many people. If I had to guess, I would think this hits men even harder than women. You can probably use this approach more with private individuals. In B2B business, in price discussions with companies, there is less "ego" involved, at least in this regard. It's less about what you can afford and more about budgets.

71. ***Sorry, I thought you had the appropriate financial resources.***

This variant of objection-handling in a sales conversation is like the previous one and is just as hard. Use it, if at all, only with a great deal of tact and if you know exactly what you are doing.

72. ***You can then also tell everyone what a great product you have bought.***

Enhancing our external image with things we can afford is an extremely widespread need, although few would admit it. You address this reaction to the customer's price objection directly. Hardly any customer, when asked, would admit that this kind of status is important to them. But accepting this as a statement and leaving it uncommented on or unchallenged in the room is possible without being superficial.

73. ***What do you think your neighbors (colleagues, customers, etc.) will say or think when they see you wearing it?***

This question is in the same vein as the previous statement. It can also be used to preempt post-purchase loyalty, for example, "What do you think your partner will say when you get home with this?" You bring the status that the product confers into play but in a very indirect way. "They'll be amazed," you might elicit from the customer. But the answer is not so crucial. What's more decisive is the insinuation that the neighbors will be amazed and perhaps even a little envious, which resonates in the question.

74. ***You'll probably get it for a lower price in a few months, but then you will no longer be the first.***

With this, you are saying a fact that is true in many fields. Products are initially more expensive to take advantage of the urge of customers who want to be among the first to own that product. This pricing strategy is also known as "price skimming" or skimming strategy. The choice remains with the customer, of course, but if the need to be among the first is strong enough, they will buy despite the "too high" price.

75. *Do you want to boast that you brought in a cheap consultant?*

It's exciting that there are areas where customers boast that they have bought particularly cheaply and others where the exact opposite is the case; the more expensive the better. This is particularly common in the luxury goods segment. But people also brag about personal services, for example, how expensive a certain doctor, hairdresser, or consultant was. Hardly any responsible manager will say, "As you all know, we are currently in a very difficult situation with our sales organization. Fortunately, I managed to bring in a very cheap consultant!"

REVERSE LOGIC

Creating confusion can sometimes be a good tactic for dealing with objections in a price discussion. It throws your counterpart off balance and away from any planned strategy. And you cause confusion, for example, by making statements that the customer does not expect and that sound completely illogical the first time they hear them. On closer inspection, for you must then explain these statements in your objection handling; however, there is a reverse and thoroughly convincing logic in these statements or questions.

76. *That's exactly why you should buy it.*

This response to "too expensive" is like verbal judo. Like judo, you use the energy of the objection for yourself and turn it into an argument that speaks for your offer. You won't succeed with every price objection, but when you do, it's very effective. If you use this strategy then, of course, you must have a suitable explanation for the statement. You will rarely come up with one on the spur of the moment, and certainly not an excellent one, so preparation is particularly important in this case.

77. *I made it that way especially for you.*

This statement in response to "too expensive" will astonish your customer. The subsequent explanation could, for example, be that the customer values high quality and this has its price. As with No. 76, preparing a good explanation is a prerequisite for using these variants.

78. *I also have a guilty conscience about asking so much money from you, but that's nothing compared to the guilty conscience I would have if I offered you something cheaper.*

Here, too, the question is, "Why would you, as a salesperson, have a guilty conscience about offering the customer something cheap?" The answer is obvious, cheap is synonymous with bad and often causes problems for the customer afterward. From this point of view, you are doing them a favor by offering the higher-priced product.

Picture: Shutterstock

79. **Your money is currently yielding approx. 0% in the bank. These products increase in value by about 5% a year. So, the more money you put into these products and the less you have in the bank, the better for you.**

As strange as this argument sounds in a price negotiation, it is not without a certain logic and could absolutely be used to deal with objections in some situations and for certain products. It is a combination of a business argument and a somewhat paradoxical approach to objection-handling.

80. **That's right. I want to save you the trouble you would have if you bought something cheap.**

Clear and direct, the message here is, "Buy something decent, or you'll be in trouble." And something decent costs more money. Everyone understands that immediately. But the reversal in this form of objection treatment makes you think. The implicit argumentation again follows the line that cheaper products will bring you problems, and I want to avoid them in your life.

81. **Can you afford to buy something cheap?**

Can you afford to buy something expensive? Everyone understands that immediately. But the reversal in this form of objection treatment makes you think. The implicit argumentation again follows the line that cheaper products bring you problems and I want to avoid them for you. The statement, "We can't afford anything cheaper" was used for a while by Bluestar, a WC cleaner—a sign that this can be used quite sensibly.

CLOSING ORIENTATION

Objections, especially price objections, are a closing signal. The customer is at least indicating that they are interested and might be willing to buy. With this category of variants for dealing with objections, you will increase the speed towards closing the deal and even use the objection to directly ask a closing question, if necessary.

82. *I see! That means you'd rather have the cheaper one?*

The word that matters in this response is "have." This makes the question a direct closing question. If you leave out the "have" and just say something like, "Would you prefer the cheaper version?" the question does not have this effect and is not yet a closing question. If the customer answers No. 82 in the affirmative they are clearly saying, "I want this!"

83. *Why would you still buy it?*

This is also a variant with role reversal (see above), but this time with significantly more traction to the conclusion. Again, the exact wording is important, especially the word "buy." Herein lies the presupposition that there are other arguments that compensate for the too-high price. If you formulate the question, for example, as, "What reasons are there still for your choice?" it is not a closing question.

84. *Does that mean that if we agree on the price, I will get the order from you?*

This is one of the best ways of dealing with objections in price negotiations. In this way, you ensure that the customer, after you have found a price solution,– will buy and not come back with three more requests or objections. You force them to clearly state what is still holding them back from buying. But beware, if you have not said by now that there is still room to maneuver on the price, do so with this question. After all, you admit that it is possible to talk about the price and then agree on this.

85. *What screw, apart from the price, can we turn to get you to say yes?*

Hidden in this question is another presupposition, namely that there are other possibilities, apart from price, that can lead to a deal. As in some of the other variants in this book, you exclude a price reduction with this question and direct the focus to other possibilities. Your customer is challenged to find some and tell you about them.

Bonus 9: Do you still want to buy/ have it?

This very direct closing question as a direct rebuttal to a price objection sounds strange, but we have all bought things despite a price that is too high. That could also be the case with your customer. If they answer "No," you can always proceed with one of the other variations. If they answer "Yes," you've taken a shortcut in the sales conversation and saved yourself a lot of discussion about price.

TOGETHER TO THE GOAL

There are always situations in sales talks in which your discussion partner cannot or does not want to decide alone because the price is too high. A next higher authority or a partner must also give their approval, or perhaps your customer simply wants to get more opinions. For exactly these cases, you will find variants of objection-handling based on the idea of closing ranks and jointly convincing the third party (boss, partner, committee, etc.).

86. *What can we do together to convince your boss (your husband/ wife/ business partner, etc.)?*

By asking this question, you transform the price negotiation from being against each other to being with each other. The new "opponent" is the boss or the wife/ husband, and this can sometimes be very bonding. This variant of objection handling works best in combination with the next one.

87. *And would you agree if it were your decision alone?*

Whenever it is not just one person who decides you can achieve stage victories with this question. You don't have a contract yet, but at least you know whose side your interlocutor is on, and you are an important step further.

88. *Then we should talk to the boss. When can we do that?*

Instead of asking at length if you can talk to the boss, simply ask when you can (a presupposition). The surprise effect plays into your hands. And if the boss is the one who decides, then it's also only natural to talk to them.

89. ***We're in the same boat—my boss wouldn't agree to a lower price either.***

Commonalities are something very unifying in interpersonal communication. Even the boss breathing down your neck can be a very unifying element. And just as your customer can have a boss who must agree, so can you. But beware, if you bring the boss card into play too often in price discussions with customers who repeatedly buy, over time, you will lose credibility as a salesperson. In the future, your customers may turn directly to the boss if you have too little or no decision-making power in price matters.

90. ***That's just as well. I have to go to the bathroom anyway. You are welcome to use my phone.***

This admittedly very cheeky variant of objection-handling is suitable if your customer says, for example, that they must still discuss the price with their spouse. It is important that you also underline this statement in body language by getting up and going to the toilet. And walking away must happen quickly, while the customer is still so surprised that they don't have an answer ready.

BODY LANGUAGE

Responding wordlessly to price objections and only using body language is sometimes much more effective than delivering the best and most eloquent arguments. Body language is more credible than words and is, therefore, quite rightly, responsible for most of the impact of our communication.

91. *Say nothing, pack up, and start walking*

Of course, if this is how you respond to your customer's price objection, you must be ready to go if the customer doesn't stop you, but it could well be that your customer stops you. And clearly, this variant is only applicable when you are physically with the customer.

This does not mean that you must jump up immediately. You could pause after packing up and switch to small talk. This is also a clear sign that the price talk is over.

92. *Shake head, look serious and sad and exhale audibly.*

This type of objection treatment can be combined well with the previous one by attaching the previous one to it. Shake your head, look sad, exhale audibly, start packing up, and leave. Again, physically leaving is only the last consequence. Before that, it is advisable to look at the customer and remain silent.

In many cases, your customer will say something in response to your body language reaction. Often this will be an explanation of their demand, but sometimes it will be an apology or justification. You also should not be surprised if your customer begins to tone down their demand. Body language strategies of this kind in combination with periods of silence are very powerful tools in communication.

TOTAL OPENNESS

If you have nothing (more) to hide, you can show it. This variant of objection handling is very suitable if you have such tight margins or contribution margins that your customer immediately refrains from any further requests for a better price.

93.	***Disclose the calculation for the customer***

This approach is naturally limited to a few areas of application. I experienced this when I asked for a bulk discount in an electronics store when buying three video cameras. After the salesman showed me his screen and gave me insight into his margins, I backed off from my request and bought anyway. However, I hope your margins are not so low that you can resort to this approach too often.

ARGUMENTATION

In this category, you will find a collection of different arguments that can suit a wide variety of situations. The dangerous thing about using arguments in objection-handling is that they are often "counter-arguments" and thus reinforce the confrontation.

If you, as a salesperson, want to prove to the customer that they are wrong with their price objection (à la "That's not true; compared with XY, our offer is cheaper!"), you can easily end up in a dead end. After all, who likes to be wrong? Therefore, if you want to use classic arguments, you must use them with a lot of tact. You must not appear confrontational.

94. ***I'm glad you said that! Let me tell you a short story about this.***

Instead of arguing against it, in this variant of objection-handling, you tell a story that supports your point of view. You don't say the customer is wrong with their price demand but let them draw their own conclusions based on the story. What you need for this, of course, are good short stories and examples that contain the message you want to convey.

95. ***From my personal experience, the pain of separation from the money we spend on high quality is a short one. We enjoy the pleasure of the great product for a lifetime, day after day.***

Telling about your personal experience is a gentle way to bring other perspectives into play. You could also support this version with a story about a personal experience. You may even have a product with you that can serve as an example.

96. ***Yes, everything is getting more expensive. The other day, I happened to have the ten-year-old bill from my washing machine in my hands and realized that I had paid twice as much for the new one.***

You can use this kind of objection-handling especially if your customer is in a similar situation and they are comparing with a previous purchase. The compound interest effect of the inflation rate is often underestimated, and ten years can make a huge difference in absolute price alone, even though it is the same as before relative to income or even cheaper.

If you want to strengthen this argument even more, then calculate inflation based on your figures. For a period of, say, ten years and an inflation rate of 2% per year, that alone adds up to over 21%. This does not even consider the fact that the product you are offering today is probably much better and offers more than it did ten years ago.

97. ***In my experience, the more I invest in things that I really like, the more satisfied I am with my decision in the long run.***

And another variation with a personal experience that emphasizes a long-lasting good feeling versus the short pain of loss.

98. ***That's less than what you spend on XY each month.***

All people have areas where money is looser and easier to spend than in others. And this difference often cannot be rationally explained in any meaningful way. We are happy when we can save a few cents per liter on gas and accept detours to do so.

On the other hand, in other areas, we quickly spend 100 or even 1,000 euros more than planned. You point this out more or less discreetly. Make sure, however, that your objection-handling does not come across as reproachful. You can also phrase this variation as a question, "What do you spend significantly more on per month?"

PRAISE

P raise (in the form of attribution of behaviors) can be a very effective tool in objection-handling. When you praise your customer for a behavior you would like to see in them (whether they already exhibit it or not), you put them on a pedestal from which they will find it very difficult to push themselves down. This approach is known in behavioral psychology as the labeling technique.

99. *Fortunately, you are someone who can distinguish between "expensive" and "too expensive" very well.*

Your customer can hardly contradict this attribution directly. And, of course, you trust they will see your offer as "expensive," but not "too expensive."

100. *Therefore, we sell only to people like you, who are also willing to spend a little more money for the best quality.*

Again, you implicitly imply that your offering equates to "best quality" and praise the customer for their willingness to invest in quality.

101. *That's why I'm very glad that there are people like you who can also afford something like this.*

In this form of objection-handling, you praise your customer for their economic potency. Who can argue with that?

SELF-CONFIDENT, CHEEKY, AND IMPUDENT

These ways of responding to your customer's "too expensive" (especially the cheeky and impertinent ones) require an extremely good relationship level with the customer in order not to annoy them or risk your expulsion. But introduced with a little tact and a wink of the eye, these variants of objection-handling can lighten up the situation a bit and show limits in a humorous way, particularly if your customer makes demands that range from impertinent to outrageous, the below reactions on your part are absolutely fine and appropriate.

102. *Do you want a cheap supplier? I can gladly name someone for you!*

Here you go one step further and go on the offensive. Instead of just saying that you are not a low-cost provider, you even name such to your customer. This can be disarming. I have never heard of a customer accepting the offer with thanks. When phrasing your question, the word "cheap" should have a slightly pejorative undertone to clearly distinguish it from "cheap" and clearly mark it as bad.

103. *Absolutely right! If you want something cheap, you are at the wrong address.*

Not cheeky, but self-confident and a very clear statement. It is always interesting to observe how attractive the salesperson and their offer become through such an openly displayed self-confident attitude. With this and similar approaches, you turn the game around: Instead of wanting to sell the customer something at all costs, they may buy from you—but only if they are willing to pay the price.

104. *Why do you waste your time and mine if you want to buy something cheap?*

This is stronger stuff and includes the possibility that your customer will break off the price discussion at this point. However, if formulated objectively and clearly, this variant can be used in certain situations. If you want to formulate this question a little more gently, you can do it thus: "Why are we (instead of you) wasting our time when you want to buy something cheaper (instead of cheap)?" This way you are no longer blaming the customer alone for wasting your time.

105. *Do you want to buy a product or discount?*

It's interesting to see how important discounts are in some areas. At the regulars' table, people brag about who got more discount when buying a car. The actual price or even the product is often talked about much less.

I even know from some buyers in larger organizations that they are often primarily looking for a discount. This also has to do with the criteria by which they are judged. The above question is especially applicable in situations where the focus is not so much on price but on discount.

With this question, you move the focus back to where it belongs - on the product. Many customers will feel caught out and (at least tacitly) agree with you.

Customer: How much of a discount do you offer?
Seller: You can choose the one you want. I will then calculate the right price for you?
Picture: Fotolia 208358819 S

106. ***And how much discount do you want? You can choose it. I will then calculate the appropriate price for you.***

Exaggeration is a communication technique often used to get things moving in deadlocked situations such as price negotiations. With this paradoxical, almost ridiculous-looking offer, you pillory the tactic used in some industries of offering ridiculously high discounts on massively inflated prices. In doing so, you distance yourself from it and underline your seriousness.

107. ***Are you warm too? (If the customer says nothing but groans).***

Humor also helps in price negotiations. Especially when the going gets hot, a pinch of humor can help you get one step further. In this type of objection-handling, you use reframing and interpret the customer's groaning, due to the price, as a sign that your customer is too warm.

108. ***I have calculated the prices, not estimated/ diced!***

A cheeky but very pointed reaction to cheeky or outrageous price demands from your customer. If you think this approach would be too cheeky and not practical, I must disappoint you. The salesman from whom I learned this variant uses it successfully. Not always, but often. As mentioned at the beginning, if the situation and the relationship with the customer fit, all variants can be used.

Saleswoman: Sorry! - I have calculated the prices and not diced!
Customer: Can you offer a discount on the price?
Picture: Fotolia 96616339 S

109. *That's a good one! I know a good one, too: A Rabbi and a Priest meet ...*

You can use this to counter your customer's exaggerated discount demands. Through this reframing, you interpret their demand as a joke and make them understand that you are not taking the demand seriously. In response, start telling a joke yourself. Make sure it is a short but good one. In this way, you simultaneously bring humor back into the price conversation. Such an approach often "cleans" the situation, and you can continue your conversation with your customer on a different basis afterward.

110. *I am sorry, but I have nothing to give away.*

This is the end! Said in a pointed way, this response to a price demand can be used in price negotiations if your customer's demands are too high. For this statement to be credible and thus effective, it is important that you underline it with your body language, for example, lean back and close your documents.

111. *Oh, is it your birthday? I did not know that!*

Presented with a twinkle in your eye, this type of objection-handling is likely to elicit a smile from your customer and lighten up a potentially tense situation in the price negotiation.

112. *Christmas has gone already, but now seriously*

And here's another humorous way to tell your customer that their asking price is too high and bring them back to more realistic ideas.

Bonus 10: I wonder if there's anything I can do about the price? Sure. For example, I could color the zeros in green and the eights in blue. That looks very good—at least that's what my customers say.

You can use this variant as an answer to the customer's question about whether something is still possible at the price. You can do this with a wink or remain serious if it's appropriate. In any case, you need a very good relationship level; otherwise, this approach may lead to the termination of the conversation.

Bonus 11: Yes, there is always room for improvement.

This deliberate misinterpretation of the customer's question as to whether there is still something possible in the price or whether it is still feasible is usually made with a wink to indicate that it is not meant quite seriously. In essence, however, it is a very serious statement: There is no discount on this price.

QUOTES AND SAYINGS

Proverbs accompany us in many situations in life and give simple and practical instructions for action. So, why not use sayings and quotes in objection-handling? Some sayings would also fit into the previous category and vice versa.

However, sayings can sometimes come across as trite; therefore, choose well which ones you use and when you use them.

Picture: Fotolia 121963390 S

113. *There will always be something cheaper.*

In doing so, you are clearly stating that your goal is not to be the cheapest but to be the best, most innovative, most likable, etc. This response to a price objection from your customer also says that you will not make any further effort to accommodate them on price.

114. *Do you know what EXPENSIVE stands for? Great, unique, incomparable, exquisite, and right for you*

Acronyms, special forms of abbreviation, are common and popular. They make it easier to remember things or to formulate them more pointedly. So why not use an acronym in objection-handling? In this form, the acronym is associated with reframing. Expensive becomes something positive.

115. *Wilhelm Busch has already said, "On closer inspection, the price often also increases the respect!"*

Very old and still very good, this saying says in principle the same as the next, only more beautifully formulated. Wilhelm Busch used this saying to explain the reverse price elasticity.

Simply put, in many product and service areas we infer high quality from a high price. But higher prices also have a positive effect on status. Status increases in the eyes of others, and also in our eyes, if something we own or use is known to be expensive.

116. *You know how it is, what costs nothing is worth nothing.*

This is a variant of the objection-handling in the price discussion which expresses the same as the previous one but is formulated more directly and is easier to understand.

117. *Quality never comes at a discount.*

This quote contains two important messages. First: It is a quality product or service. And secondly: no discount is possible.

118. *If you buy cheap, you buy expensive. But you know that.*

The idea of this saying, equating lower prices with poorer quality, has already been taken up in several variants of objection-handling in this book. However, it can be communicated more pointedly in the form of a saying. In addition, your customer may have used exactly this saying many times.

THE BEST OBJECTION-HANDLING

So, what's the best way to handle price objections? I'm asked this repeatedly. The answer is, "The one you don't have to use." The best way to counter price objections is to not let them arise in the first place.

And you can do that by positioning yourself or your company and designing your offer in such a way that you avoid comparability via price altogether. Price objections arise primarily when the customer has no other criteria with which to compare. From this point of view, sellers sometimes force their customers to compare prices.

The path to high prices, contribution margins, margins, and profits is not just a question of skillful negotiation in price talks. For individual entrepreneurs, especially self-employed service providers, it moves through eight stages, or nine stages for medium-sized or larger companies, of which price negotiation and dealing with price objections is the last.

The preceding stages are decisive for whether a price negotiation takes place at all and at which price level it starts.

"Customers who pay the most pay the most attention."

As far as I know, this quote comes from the American entrepreneur Alex Hormozi. At least, I read it in one of his books. Since it sounds and works much better in English, I have not translated it. It has much more depth and meaning than he suggests at first glance. It is not so much something you can, or mostly should, bring up in response to a price objection. Rather, it is a quote for you as a salesperson and, in my opinion, a very good conclusion to this collection of answers to price objections.

It is those customers who spend a lot of money with you who most appreciate what you offer or do. Again, it shows that what costs nothing is worth nothing. But it also usually applies to those customers who use your offer most intensively and derive the most benefits from it because it is valuable to you. If you offer services such as coaching or consulting, you will often also find that these clients implement the most from it and change the fastest. So, in many cases, high prices and fees are not only good for you but also very directly good for the client. So do yourself and your client a favor and sell at high prices AND inspire the client by giving them something in return that is ultimately worth much more than what they paid for it.

Good luck

ABOUT THE AUTHOR

Marketing and pricing expert Roman Kmenta has been active internationally for more than 30 years as an entrepreneur, keynote speaker, and bestselling author. The business economist and serial entrepreneur provides his many years of international marketing and sales experience in the B2B and B2C sectors today to over 100 top companies as well as many small businesses and sole proprietors in Germany, Switzerland, and Austria.

More than 25,000 people read his blog or listen to his podcast every week. With his presentations, he provides thought-provoking impulses for salespeople, executives, and entrepreneurs on the topic of "profitable growth" and provides inspiration for his listeners and readers in the direction of a value-oriented sales and marketing approach.

www.romankmenta.com

Picture: Matern, Vienna

Perfect for international sales organizations

1 book in 23 languages

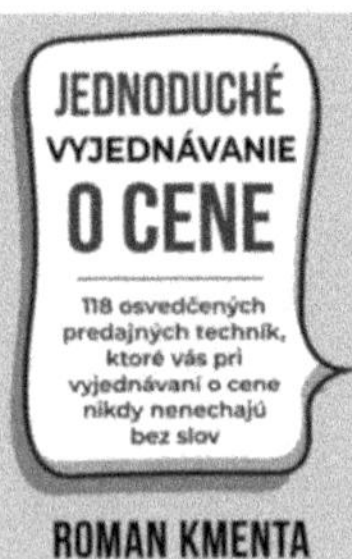

For more information:
https://www.romankmenta.com/buch-zu-teuer-international/

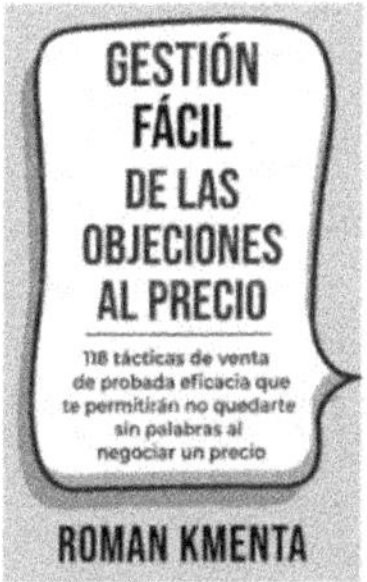

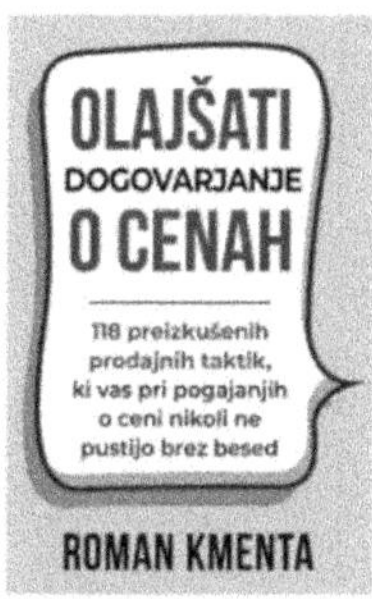

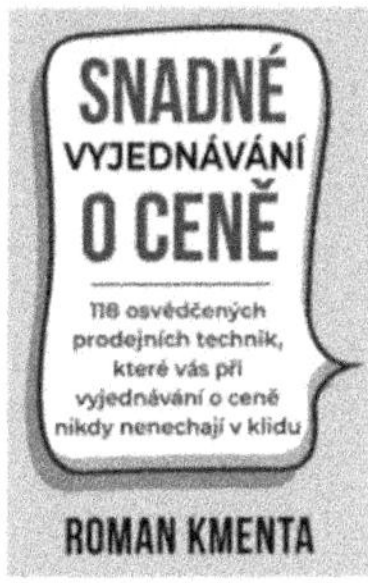

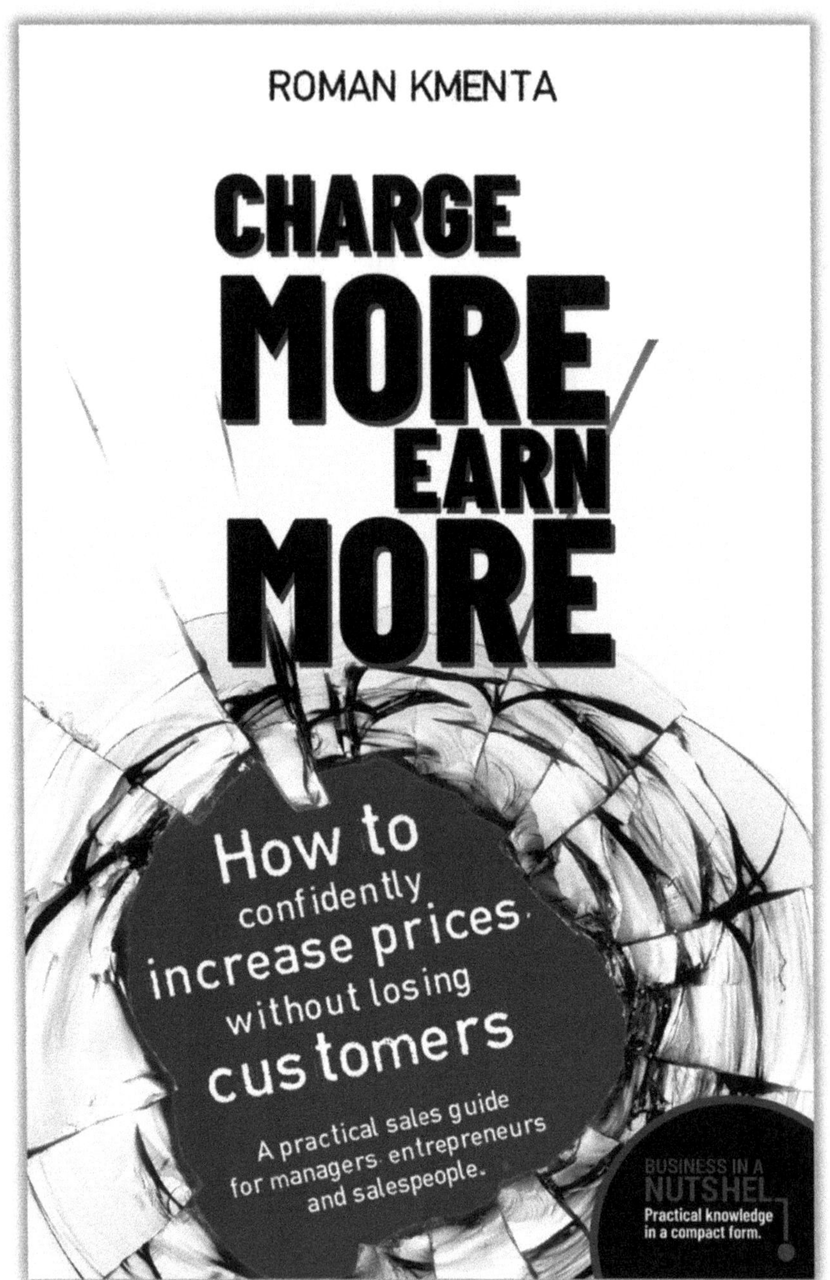

ROMAN KMENTA
CHARGE
MORE
EARN
MORE
How to
confidently
increase prices
without losing
customers
A practical sales guide
for managers, entrepreneurs
and salespeople.
BUSINESS IN A
NUTSHEL
Practical knowledge
in a compact form.

Charge more earn more

Top strategies to enforce higher prices!

Achieving higher prices is a key success factor for most companies. A very special challenge is to carry out price increases with existing customers in such a way that the customer remains a customer. It is important to know about and implement a number of decisive strategies in sales and marketing.

This book is dedicated to these strategies. Pricing and price increases are issues that affect the entire company. Roman Kmenta 84 Accordingly, some of the recommended approaches are comprehensive, far-reaching, and in-depth. At the same time, you will also find tips in this book that can be implemented quickly and easily, which will make the next price increase easier and bring you a lot of money.

In this book you will learn:

- when the optimal time is for a price increase
- how not to make a price increase look like one
- how to avoid price comparability
- how to increase the value of your offer in the eyes of the customer
- how to avoid price negotiations
- which price psychological affects you should be aware of
- which arguments you can use to support a price increase
- how to raise prices without raising prices.

Higher prices, higher contribution margins, and more income.

A book that pays off.

www.romankmenta.com/shop

ROMAN KMENTA
HOW TO WRITE OFFERS THAT SELL
44
psychological strategies to create a successful offer
A practical sales guide for managers, entrepreneurs and salespeople
BUSINESS IN A NUTSHEL
Practical knowledge in a compact form.

How to write offers that sell

44 psychological strategies to create a sucessful offer!

Written offers are a greatly underestimated instrument in the sales process. A lot of companies produce many of them, but pay little attention to them. Offers are silent salespeople, who spend more time with or at the customer, than the sales force in some business areas and industries.

So how can you raise the potential that lurks in your offers and turn them into better sellers? How can you design your offers to convince your customers?

In this book you will learn:

- why your customers basically don't care about your offer and what they are really interested in
- how to build up offers effectively in terms of sales psychology
- how your offers can be made much more attractive with the right design
- what the most promising ways of delivering your offers are
- which price psychological strategies you use to make your offers appear more favorable
- how you clearly differentiate yourself from your competitors through your offers
- what a "Shock and Awe Package" is and how you can use it in a targeted manner.

Better offers bring more sales to a close.

A book that pays off.
www.romankmenta.com/shop

The Keynote Speech
for your next Event

"Not at any Price -
A Plea for Value in Times of Cheapness"

Keynote Speaker Roman Kmenta will bring motivation to executives, entrepreneurs, salespeople and distributors at your next event.

For bookings please contact:
service@romankmenta.com
www.romankmenta.com

"He was just super! Really, really great. He was excellent in both content and rhetoric. His humorous interludes and stories perfectly rounded off the presentation ."

Karin Furtner, CEO Frau in der Wirtschaft Wirtschaftskammer Vorarlberg